The First and the Last

- - - - -

The First and the Last

- - - - -

By

Isaiah Berlin

Introduced by

Henry Hardy

Tributes by

NOEL ANNAN

STUART HAMPSHIRE

AVISHAI MARGALIT

BERNARD WILLIAMS

AILEEN KELLY

NEW YORK REVIEW BOOKS

New York

"'The Purpose Justifies the Ways'" and "My Intellectual Path"
are reproduced by permission of Curtis Brown Ltd., London,
on behalf of The Isaiah Berlin Literary Trust
Copyright © 1998 The Isaiah Berlin Literary Trust and Henry Hardy

Tributes:
Copyright © 1998 Noel Annan
Copyright © 1998 Stuart Hampshire
Copyright © 1998 Avishai Margalit
Copyright © 1998 Bernard Williams
Copyright © 1998 Aileen Kelly

The First and the Last Copyright © 1999 NYREV, Inc.

All rights reserved

Published in 1999 in the United States of America by
The New York Review of Books
1755 Broadway, New York, NY 10019

Front cover photography:
© The Isaiah Berlin Literary Trust 1998
Back cover photography:
© Sharon Collins, 1999/Nonstock

Library of Congress Cataloging-in-Publication Data
Berlin, Isaiah, Sir.
    [Purpose justifies the ways]
    The first and the last / by Isaiah Berlin; introduced by Henry Hardy;
tributes by Noel Annan . . . [et al.].
        p.   cm.
    Includes bibliographical references.
    Contents: The purpose justifies the ways—My intellectual path.
    ISBN 0-940322-09-9 (hardcover: alk. paper)
    1. Berlin, Isaiah, Sir. 2. Soviet Union—History—Revolution,
1917–1921 Personal narratives. I. Annan, Noel Gilroy Annan, Baron,
1916–   . II. Berlin, Isaiah, Sir. My intellectual path.
III. Title.
B1618.B453P87   1999
192—dc 21   99-26531
                                                            CIP

Printed in the United States of America on acid-free paper
October 1999

www.nybooks.com

Contents

- - - - -

Acknowledgment

- - - - -

"My Intellectual Path" was written for a volume edited by Ouyang Kang and Steve Fuller, *Contemporary British and American Philosophy and Philosophers*, to be published first in Chinese translation by The People's Press, Beijing, and subsequently in English.

The First
and
the Last

- - - - -

FOLLOWING

ARE THE

FIRST KNOWN PIECE

AND THE LAST ESSAY

WRITTEN BY

ISAIAH BERLIN,

WHO DIED ON

NOVEMBER 5, 1997

Isaiah Berlin

- - - - -

"The Purpose Justifies the Ways"

Isaiah Berlin came to England in early 1921, aged eleven, with virtually no English. This story (untitled in the manuscript), which according to Berlin won "a hamper of tuck" in a children's magazine competition, was written in February 1922, when he was twelve; it is signed "I. Berlyn" at the end. As far as is known, it is his earliest surviving extended piece of writing, as well as his only story, and shows how far his English had developed after just a year. It appears here in an exact transcription, apart from a few trivial alterations where total fidelity might hold the reader up.

Moise Solomonovich Uritsky, Commissar for Internal Affairs in the Northern Region Commune of Soviet Russia, and Chairman of the Petrograd Cheka, was murdered by a member of the Russian gentry named

Kunnegiesser on August 31, 1918. Uritsky's "motto" has been chosen as the title because it signals the way in which the story points forward to Berlin's repeated later insistence on the inadmissibility of justifying present suffering as a route to some imaginary future state of bliss. In this sense the story is the first recorded step on his intellectual journey through life, a journey summarized in his last essay, "My Intellectual Path," written seventy-four years later in 1996, which is also published in this volume.

Berlin always ascribed his lifelong horror of violence, especially when ideologically inspired, to an episode he witnessed at the age of seven during the February Revolution in Petrograd in 1917: while out walking he watched a policeman loyal to the tsar, white-faced with terror, being dragged off by a lynch mob to his death. This story surely vividly reflects the power of this early experience.

HENRY HARDY

THE STORY OF which I am going to tell is about the murder of Uritzky minister of justice of soviet Russia in the y. 1918. already in the year 1918 the people in Russia and its Capital Petrograd especially, were very depressed by the Bolshevicks who terrorized the people to the utmost. One of the most noble families in Petrograd was the family of the Ivanov's. It consisted of Andrew Ivanov an old man aged 64, his son Peter a handsome and brave young man, and an old servant named Vasily. although very depressed they had a cozy little home in which peace and friendships reigned undisturbed until a sudden shock came about to destroy their well earned happiness. It was a bright cold winter morning the sun appeared as a little red disc on the clear sky. all nature seemed to be enjoying itself lapped by the bright rays of the sun. A sudden knock at the door was heard and the next moment an officer and two soldiers entered Ivanovs' little hall.

Is Andrew Ivanov living here? asked the officer curtly

I am Andrew Ivanov and am at your service answered the old man quitly—

"take him away" ordered the officer signing to his soldiers—"this man is guilty before the law for hiding some diamonds in his house, search the house instantly and if you find any precious stones you will give them to me.* Peter who looked at the scene with bewilderment and anger suddenly dealt the officer a blow that send him on to the floor while himself quick as a lightning jumped out of the window and soon was out of sight. The soldiers followed the example of their commander

---

*Once when the Berlins' flat in Petrograd was searched the maid successfully hid the few family jewels in the snow on the balcony.

who rose from the ground and went for Peter. But the Blow over his head made him fall over the first stone that lay in his way and thus stopped him. In his fall a sheet of paper fell out of his hip pocket. Old Vasili the servant who followed him, remarkably quickly for a man of 60 picked up the paper unnoticed by the officer.

II

- - - - -

MEANWHILE PETER DECIDED to go to his cousin Leonid. Leonid a young man himself five years elder than his cousin was dining when Peter rushed in. His burning black eyes, wavang dark hair and the bewildered expression on his countenanse made Leonid stunned to his place amazed and bewildered.

Where do yo come from cousin? he asked when

he Recovered his breath, and what does that wild
look of yours mean?—

Peter, full of hatred told everything briefly to
Leonid when a knock on the door interrupt him—
"the soldiers!" exclaimed Peter who looked
through the keyhole—

this way pointed Leonid shortly pointing at the
cupboard in the room—

Peter jumped into it without any noise. Leonid
who opened the door to the soldiers let them in and
as if amazed asked what made you enter my quit
house my worthy friends?

The deceived soldiers asked in loud voices:
"Leonid Ivanov confess that your cousin is hiding
here you will not be remmembered in the court as a
guilty man for we know all your little faults for
which you deserve to be punished

Peter trembled in his hiding place when he
heared this—

No my worthy friends you are on the wrong
path and very much mistaken in thinking that Peter
my cousin is here. He never entered my house since

his last visit two weeks ago. Leonid played his part so well that the soldiers were ready to believe that they made mistake—

But we saw Peter enter this house . . . in any case you would not mind if we would search the house instantly

But my friends Protested Leonid, surly you would not mind a glass of good wine before you start!

ahoy! Gregory bring some of my best wine for these worthy veterans, cried Leonid not waiting for the answer of the soldiers now then friends let us be merry

Leonid all the time added more and more wine to the cups of the "comrades" while himself hardly touched his own cup. Two hours passed and the drunken soldiers were carried off to unconscious Meanwhile Peter thanked Leonid for his narrow escape, when suddenly Vasily the old servant of the Ivanovs rushed in

your father is murdered by the wretches exclaimed the man by the order of Uritzky and there is the evidence said vasily hastily pulling out of his pocket the document he picked up when the officer dropped it. It run like this

"BY THE HAND OF URITZKY MINISTER OF JUSTICE IN THE REPUBLIC OF THE SOLDIER'S PEASANT'S AND WORKMEN'S DEPUTIES.

ALLOWANCE GIVEN TO CAPTAIN B. TO ARREST ANDREW IVANOV AND IF NEC-ESSARY ALSO PETER IVANOV.

URITZKY

when Peter had read this he found a bit of paper between the folds of the document

"ANDREW IVANOV TO BE SHOT 3.15 P.M. AT THE GOROHOVAYA 3. PETER IVANOV TO BE EXECUTED AT 5.30 THE SAME DAY

URITZKY

Peter looked at his watch it showed 3.10 p.m. without telling a word he darted from the house in the direction of Gorohovaya 3. he entered the gate at 3.14 ½.

30 seconds remained not looking where he went he slipped and fell down when he got up he heard a horrible scream, death and life fought in this scream boom twelve guns sounded and Peter knew the fate of his father. he wondered on the streets like a madman at last when he came back to Leonids house he fainted on the doorstep Leonid at once understood what had happened he tried to keep himself up but failed and burst into bitter tears

after Peter came to his senses again the old Vasily said to him Peter! thy enemies the BOLSHEvist wretches have executed thy father! therefore swear theat thou wilt revenge for thy father!—

in that minute a shot was fired through the window by the officer which came to know how his soldiers were treated he fired to revenge himself for the blow he received his shot hit Vasily in his back.

I swear! said Peter meanwhile the old man's eyes

for a moment closed opened and had that clear
look that people only get in their last moments

revenge! he murmured and fell heavily on Peters
hands unconscious a minute esllapsed and he
opened his eyes for the last time I'm going to meet
you my Master... Andr... he did not finish for
death cut his bounds on the earth

as long as I live I shall try to revenge upon
Uritzky called Peter loudly

And I am with you and Peter cried Leonid taking
a step forward and raising his hand

death to Uritzky they cried both.

- - - - -

I T   W A S   T H E   year 1919 a dark november night
the wind blew outside and the soft armchair before
the burning stove seemed so warm and comfort-
able. in this deep armchair sat a man about forty
years old with long flowing hair which showed a big
white forehead two deep little black eyes, covered
with long eyebrows grown to gether which gave his

face a somewhat severe look a sharp nose, a carnivorous mouth and a sharp chin covered with a little french beard. this was the famous Uritzky.

he possesed a clever but also cruel look and all his countenence bore an expression of a phanatic he signed death verdicts, without moving his eyebrow. his leading motto in life was "The purpose justifies the WAYS" he did not stop before anything for bringing out his plans.

He made a good impression at first but if once looked at the man with his little burning eyes the man felt that Ur. read all his thoughts his eyes made an impression of a thousand little spears shooting through one's brains.

His look hypnotised people whom he wanted to obey him. This was once a famous man "comrade" Uritzky.

The man of action

And one of the greatest BOLSHEVIST factors.

he divided manhood in two classes first class people that stood in his way, second, the people who obeyed him.

The former according to Uritzky's understanding did not deserve to live at all.

tzin! tzin! sounded the bell wrung By Uritzky. a moment later Uritzky's young secretary appeared his name was Michael SEREVEEV he wore a big black beard and a black curling moustashe, had he not the moustash and the beard which at a careful examination would be recognised as false you would see our old friend Peter Ivanov—

"sit down Michael said Ur. to him in a weak voice. After Michael alias Peter sat Uritzky continued his talk—"come here he said melancholically and tell me a story that would quiten my nerves, for I am tired of the days work, you know Michael, tell me a story that a nurse told you when you were a baby it is foolish But it will quiten my nerves go on and tell me your tale.—

I see sir answered Peter and began.

"Thousands of years ago and thousands of miles away there lived a folk of good people the people were kind and noble and enjoyed their life thoroughly until a great disaster came along a new

not worthy government ruled the country and des-
troyed it it shed the Blood of the people at the head
of it stood an ex murderer a cruel an clever villain

between others also one of the most honourable
citizens was executed his son who also was to be
executed But HE escaped and swore to revenge his
father's death upon the villain who signed the death
verdict And now finished Peter loudly pulling out
his automatic, the hour come! hands up he shouted
levelling his pistol with Uritzky's forehead boom!
sounded The pistol and Uritzky without a groan fell
heavily on the floor

Ho! ahoy! soldiers! shouted Peter and when the
soldiers appeared he faced them with his pistol. the
soldiers moved back in alarm, I killed your master
he cried, and now my mission on earth is finished
my father is executed so is Leonid both without a
trial, and I have not got anybody to live for! Oh
Father I am going to join you BOOM Fired Peter
and fell heavily over the body of his dead enemy
when the soldiers came near they found that both
were dead

Isaiah Berlin

- - - - -

MY

INTELLECTUAL

PATH

In February 1996, in his eighty-seventh year, Isaiah Berlin received a letter from Ouyang Kang, Professor of Philosophy at Wuhan University in China, inviting him to provide a summary of his ideas for translation into Chinese and inclusion in a volume designed to introduce philosophers and students of philosophy in China to contemporary Anglo-American philosophy, hitherto largely unavailable to them in Chinese.

Berlin had written nothing substantial since 1988, when his intellectual credo, "On the Pursuit of the Ideal" (a response to the award of the first Agnelli Prize for his contribution to ethics), appeared in The New York Review. *Although his intellect was undiminished, and he had continued to compose short occasional pieces, it seemed clear that—reasonably enough in his eighties—he had in effect laid down his authorial pen.*

But the Chinese project caught his imagination: he regarded this new readership as important, and felt an obligation to address it. He told the professor that he would try to write something. With a single sheet of notes before him, he dictated a first draft onto cassette. When he had approved my edited transcript, making a few final insertions and adjustments, he said, with his characteristic distaste for revisiting his own work, that he did not wish to see the piece again. It was to be the last essay he wrote.

Contributors to the volume were asked to offer guidance to readers who might wish to study their work further. Berlin simply directed them to two other essays of his, the Agnelli Prize essay and "The Apotheosis of the Romantic Will" (1975). Both are to be found in his 1990 collection, The Crooked Timber of Humanity, *reissued by Princeton University Press in 1998.*

HENRY HARDY

1

- - - - -

OXFORD PHILOSOPHY
BEFORE THE
SECOND WORLD WAR

MY INTEREST IN philosophical issues started when I was an undergraduate at Oxford in the late 1920s and early 1930s, because philosophy was part of the course which at that time a great many students in Oxford pursued. As a result of a continuing interest in this field I was appointed in 1932 to teach philosophy, and my views at that time were naturally influenced by the kind of discussions that my philosophical contemporaries held in Oxford. There were plenty of other issues in philosophy, but as it happens the topics which my colleagues and I concentrated on were the fruits of a return to empiricism which began to dominate British philosophy before the First World War, under the influence mainly of two celebrated

25

Cambridge philosophers, G. E. Moore and Bertrand Russell.

VERIFICATIONISM

The first topic which occupied our attention in the middle and late 1930s was the nature of meaning—its relation to truth and falsehood, knowledge and opinion, and in particular the test of meaning in terms of the verifiability of the propositions in which it was expressed. The impulsion toward this topic came from the members of the Vienna School, themselves disciples of Russell and greatly influenced by thinkers such as Carnap, Wittgenstein, and Schlick. The fashionable view was that the meaning of a proposition was the way in which it was verifiable—that if there was no way whatever of verifying what was being said, it was not a statement capable of truth or falsehood, not factual, and therefore either meaningless or a case of some other use of language, as seen in commands or expressions of desire, or in imaginative literature, or in other forms of expression which did not lay claim to empirical truth.

I was influenced by this school in the sense of being absorbed in the problems and theories which it generated, but I never became a true disciple. I always believed that statements that could be true or false or plausible or dubious or interesting, while indeed they did relate to the world as empirically conceived (and I have never conceived of the world in any other way, from then to the present day), were nevertheless not necessarily capable of being verified by some simple knockdown criterion, as the Vienna School and their logical positivist followers asserted. From the beginning I felt that general propositions were not verifiable in that way. Statements, whether in ordinary use or in the natural sciences (which were the ideal of the Vienna School), could be perfectly meaningful without being strictly verifiable. If I said "All swans are white," I would never know if I knew this about all the swans there were, or whether the number of swans might not be infinite; a black swan no doubt refuted this generalization, but its positive verification in the full sense seemed to me unattainable; nevertheless it would be absurd to say that it had no meaning. The same was true about hypothetical propositions, and still more so about unfulfilled hypotheticals, of which it was plainly paradoxical to maintain that they could be shown to be true or false by empirical observation; yet they were clearly meaningful.

I thought of a great many other statements of this kind, which clearly had meaning in the full sense of the word, but whose meaning escaped the narrow criterion proposed, that of direct empirical observation—the world of the senses. Consequently, though I took a lively part in these discussions (indeed, what later came to be called Oxford Philosophy began in my rooms in the evenings, at gatherings attended by such later celebrated philosophers as A. J. Ayer, J. L. Austin, and Stuart Hampshire, influenced as they all were by

Oxford empiricism, and to some degree by Oxford realism—that is, the belief that the external world is independent of human observers), nevertheless I remained a heretic, though a friendly one. I have never departed from the views I held at that time, and still believe that while empirical experience is all that words can express—that there is no other reality—nevertheless verifiability is not the only, or indeed the most plausible, criterion of knowledge or beliefs or hypotheses. This has remained with me for the rest of my life, and has colored everything else that I have thought.

Another topic which I offered for the attention of my young colleagues was the status of such propositions as "This pink (shade) is more like this vermilion than it is like this black." If generalized, it was clear that this was a truth which no experience was likely to refute—the relations of visible colors being fixed. At the same time the general proposition could not be called a priori because it did not proceed formally from any definitions, and did not therefore belong to the formal disciplines of logic or mathematics, in which alone a priori propositions, then regarded as tautologies, belong. So we had found a universal truth in the empirical sphere. What were the definitions of "pink," "vermilion," and the rest? They had none. The colors could be recognized only by looking, so that their definitions were classified as ostensive, and from such definitions nothing logically followed. This came close to the old problem of Kant's synthetic a priori propositions, and we discussed this and its analogues for many months. I was convinced that my proposition was, if not strictly a priori, self-evidently true, and that its contradictory was not intelligible. Whether my colleagues ever raised the matter again I do not know, but the topic entered formally into the discussions held by us at the time. It corresponded to a view of Russell's embodied in a work called *The Limits of Empiricism.*

PHENOMENALISM

The other main topic that my contemporaries discussed was phenomenalism—that is, the question of whether human experience was confined to that provided by the senses, as was taught by the British philosophers Berkeley and Hume (and in some of their writings by Mill and Russell), or whether there existed a reality independent of sensible experience. For some philosophers, like Locke and his followers, there was such a reality, although it was not directly accessible to us—a reality which caused the sensible experiences which are all that we can directly know. Other philosophers held that the external world was a material reality which could be perceived directly, or misperceived as the case might be: this was called realism, as opposed to the view that our world was entirely created by human faculties—reason, imagination, and the like—which was called idealism, in which I never believed. I have never believed in any metaphysical truths—whether rationalist truths, as expounded by Descartes, Spinoza, Leibniz, and, in his own very different fashion, Kant, or the truths of (objective) idealism, the fathers of which are Fichte, Friedrich Schelling, and Hegel, who still have their disciples. Thus meaning, truth, and the nature of the external world were the topics which I thought about, and to some extent wrote about—and some of my views on them have been published.[1]

One of the intellectual phenomena which made the greatest impact on me was the universal search by philosophers for absolute certainty, for answers which could not be doubted, for total intellectual security. This from the very beginning appeared to me to be an illusory quest. No matter how solidly based, widespread, inescapable, "self-evident" a conclusion or a direct datum may seem to be, it is always possible to conceive that something could modify or indeed upset it, even if one cannot at the moment imagine what this might be. And this

---

1. See the author's *Concepts and Categories: Philosophical Essays* (Viking, 1979).

suspicion that a great deal of philosophy was set on an illusory path later came to dominate my ideas in a quite new and different connection.

While thus engaged in teaching and discussing the kind of philosophy I have outlined, I was commissioned to write a biography of Karl Marx. Marx's philosophical views never appeared to me to be particularly original or interesting, but my study of his views led me to investigate his predecessors, in particular the French *philosophes* of the eighteenth century—the first organized adversaries of dogmatism, traditionalism, religion, superstition, ignorance, oppression. I acquired an admiration for the great task which the thinkers of the *Encyclopédie* had set themselves, and for the great work which they did to liberate men from darkness—clerical, metaphysical, political, and the like. And although I came in due course to oppose some of the bases of their common beliefs, I have never lost my admiration for and sense of solidarity with the Enlightenment of that period: what I came to be critical of, apart from its empirical shortcomings, is some of its consequences, both logical and social; I realized that Marx's dogmatism, and that of his followers, in part derived from the certainties of the eighteenth-century Enlightenment.

2

- - - - -

HISTORY OF IDEAS
AND POLITICAL THEORY

DURING THE WAR I served as a British official. When I came back to Oxford to teach philosophy, I became preoccupied with two central problems. The first was monism—the central thesis of Western philosophy from Plato to our day—and the second, the meaning and application of the notion of freedom. I devoted a good deal of time to each, and they shaped my thought for a good many years to come.

MONISM

Dazzled by the spectacular successes of the natural sciences in their own century and its predecessors, men such as Helvétius, Holbach, d'Alembert, Condillac, and propagandists of genius such as Voltaire and Rousseau, believed that, provided the right method was discovered, truth of a fundamental kind could be uncovered about social, political, moral, and personal life—truth of the kind that had scored such triumphs in the investigations of the external world. The Encyclopedists believed in scientific method as the only key to such knowledge; Rousseau and others believed in eternal truths discovered by introspective means. But however they differed, they belonged to a generation which was convinced that it was on the path to the solution of all the problems that had plagued mankind from its beginnings.

A wider thesis underlay this: namely, that to all true questions there must be one true answer and one only, all the other answers being false, for otherwise the questions cannot be genuine questions. There must exist a path which leads clear thinkers to the correct answers to these questions, as much in the moral, social, and political worlds as in that of the natural sciences, whether it is the same method or not; and once all the correct answers to the deepest moral, social, and political questions that occupy (or should occupy) mankind are put together, the result will represent the final solution to all the problems of existence. Of course, we may never attain to these answers: human beings may be too confused by their emotions, or too stupid, or too unlucky, to be able to arrive at them; the answers may be too difficult, the means may be lacking, the techniques too complicated to discover; but however this may be, provided the questions are genuine, the answers must exist. If we do not know, our successors may know; or perhaps wise men in antiquity knew; and if they did not, perhaps Adam in Paradise knew; or if he did not, the angels must know; and if even they do not know, God must know—the answers must be there.

If the answers to social, moral, and political questions are discovered, then, knowing them for what they are—the truth—men cannot fail to follow them, for they would have no temptation to do otherwise. And so a perfect life can be conceived. It may not be attainable, but in principle the conception must be capable of being formed—indeed, the possibility of discovering the only true answers to the great questions must in principle be believed in.

This creed was certainly not confined to the thinkers of the Enlightenment, though the methods recommended by others differ. Plato believed that mathematics was the route to truth, Aristotle, perhaps, that it was biology; Jews and Christians sought the answers in sacred books, in the pronouncements of divinely inspired teachers and the visions of mystics; others believed that the laboratory and mathematical methods could settle things; still others believed, like Rousseau, that only the innocent human soul, the uncorrupted child, the simple peasant would know the truth—better than the corrupt inhabitants of societies ruined by civilization. But what they all agreed about, as did their successors after the French Revolution, who may have supposed the truth more difficult to obtain than their more naive and optimistic predecessors,[2] was that the laws of historical development could be—and by then had been—discovered, that the answers to the questions of how to live and what to do—morality, social life, political organization, personal relationships—are all capable of being organized in the light of the truths discovered by the correct methods, whatever those may be.

This is a *philosophia perennis*—what men, thinkers, have believed from the pre-Socratics to all the reformers and revolutionaries of our own age. It is the central belief on which human thought has rested for two millennia. For if no true answers to

---

2. Fourier, an early socialist, and Saint-Simon believed in a scientifically organized society. For Saint-Simon it was to be headed by bankers and scientists, and inspired by artists and poets. Their successors were the French socialists, such as Cabet, Pécqueur, Louis Blanc, and the terrorist Blanqui, and, in the end, Marx and Engels and their followers.

questions exist, how can knowledge ever be attainable in any province? This was the heart of European rational, and indeed spiritual, thought for many ages. No matter that people differ so widely, that cultures differ, moral and political views differ; no matter that there is a vast variety of doctrines, religions, moralities, ideas—all the same there must somewhere be a true answer to the deepest questions that preoccupy mankind.

I do not know why I always felt skeptical about this almost universal belief, but I did. It may be a matter of temperament, but so it was.

GIAMBATTISTA VICO

What first shook me was my discovery of the works of the eighteenth-century Italian thinker Giambattista Vico. He was the first philosopher, in my view, to have conceived the idea of cultures. Vico wanted to understand the nature of historical

knowledge, of history itself: it was all very well to
lean on the natural sciences as far as the external
world was concerned, but all they could provide us
with was an account of the behavior of rocks or
tables or stars or molecules. In thinking about the
past, we go beyond behavior; we wish to understand how human beings lived, and that means
understanding their motives, their fears and hopes
and ambitions and loves and hatreds—to whom
they prayed, how they expressed themselves in
poetry, in art, in religion. We are able to do this
because we are ourselves human, and understand
our own inner life in these terms. We know how a
rock, or a table, behaves because we observe it
and make conjectures and verify them; but we do
not know why the rock wishes to be as it is—
indeed, we think it has no capacity for wishing,
or for any other consciousness. But we do know
why we are what we are, what we seek, what frus-
trates us, what expresses our inmost feelings and
beliefs; we know more about ourselves than we
shall ever know about rocks or streams.

True knowledge is knowledge of why things are as they are, not merely what they are; and the more we delve into this, the more we realize that the questions asked by the Homeric Greeks are different from the questions asked by the Romans, that the questions asked by the Romans differ from those asked in the Christian Middle Ages or in the seventeenth-century scientific culture or Vico's own eighteenth-century days. The questions differ, the answers differ, the aspirations differ; the use of language, of symbols, differs; and the answers to one set of questions do not answer, do not have much relevance to, the questions of other cultures. Of course Vico was a pious Roman Catholic, and he believed that the Church alone could provide the answers. But be that as it may, it did not prevent him from formulating the original idea that cultures differ, that what matters to a fifth-century Greek is very different from what matters to a Red Indian or a Chinese or a scientist in an eighteenth-century laboratory; and therefore their outlooks differ, and there are no universal answers to all their questions.

Of course there is a common human nature, otherwise men in one age could not understand the literature or the art of another, or, above all, its laws,
about which Vico, as a jurist, knew most. But that
did not prevent there being a wide variety of cultural experience, so that activity of one kind was
relevant to activity of some other kind within a single culture, but did not share such close links with
the parallel activity in another culture.

J. G. HERDER

Then I read a far more relevant thinker, namely
the German philosopher and poet Johann Gott-
fried Herder. Herder was not the first (his teacher,
Johann Georg Hamann, has that honor) to deny the
doctrine of his French contemporaries that there
are universal, timeless, unquestionable truths which
hold for all men, everywhere, at all times; and that
the differences are simply due to error and illusion,

for the truth is one and universal—"quod ubique, quod semper, quod ab omnibus creditum est."[3] Herder believed that different cultures gave different answers to their central questions. He was more interested in the humanities, the life of the spirit, than in the external world; and he became convinced that what was true for a Portuguese was not necessarily true for a Persian. Montesquieu had begun to say this kind of thing, but even he, who believed that men were shaped by environment, by what he called "climate," was in the end a universalist—he believed that the central truths were eternal, even if the answers to local and ephemeral questions might be different. Herder laid it down that every culture possesses its own "center of gravity"[4]; each culture has its own points of reference; there is no reason why these cultures should fight each other—universal toleration must be possible—but unification

---

3. "What is believed everywhere, always, by everyone." Vincent of Lérins, *Commonitorium* 2. 3.

4. *Herders sämmtliche Werke*, edited by Bernhard Suphan (Berlin, 1877–1913), Vol. 5, p. 509.

was destruction. Nothing was worse than imperial-
ism. Rome, which crushed native civilizations in
Asia Minor in order to produce one uniform
Roman culture, committed a crime. The world was
a great garden in which different flowers and plants
grew, each in its own way, each with its own claims
and rights and past and future. From which it followed that no matter what men had in common—
and of course, again, there was a common nature
to some degree—there were no universally true
answers, as valid for one culture as for another.

Herder is the father of cultural nationalism. He
is not a political nationalist (that kind of nationalism had not developed in his time), but he believed
in the independence of cultures and the need to pre-
serve each in its uniqueness. He believed that the
desire to belong to a culture, something that united
a group or a province or a nation, was a basic
human need, as deep as the desire for food or drink
or liberty; and that this need to belong to a commu-
nity where you understood what others said, where
you could move freely, where you had emotional as

well as economic, social, and political bonds, was the basis of developed, mature human life. Herder was not a relativist, though he is often so described: he believed that there were basic human goals and rules of behavior, but that they took wholly different forms in different cultures, and that consequently, while there may have been analogies, similarities, which made one culture intelligible to another, cultures were not to be confused with each other—mankind was not one but many, and the answers to the questions were many, though there might be some central essence to them all which was one and the same.

ROMANTICISM
AND ITS OFFSPRING

This idea was developed further by the Romantics, who said something wholly new and disturbing: that ideals were not objective truths written in heaven and needing to be understood, copied, practiced by men; but that they were created by men. Values were not found, but made; not discovered, but generated—that is what some of the German Romantics certainly believed, as against the objectivist, universalizing tendency of the superficial French. Uniqueness mattered. A German poet writes poetry in German, in language which, in the course of writing, he to some degree creates: he is not simply a writer in German. The German artist is a maker of German paintings, poems, dances— and so in all other cultures. A Russian thinker, Alexander Herzen, once asked, "Where is the song before it is sung?"[5] Where indeed? "Nowhere" is the answer—one creates the song by singing it, by composing it. So, too, life is created by those who live it, step by step. This is an aesthetic interpretation of morality and of life, not an application of eternal models. Creation is all.

---

5. See A. I. Gertsen, *Sobranie sochinenii v tridtsati tomakh* (Moscow, 1954–1966), Vol. 6, pp. 33 and 335.

From this sprang all kinds of diverse movements—anarchism, Romanticism, nationalism, fascism, hero worship. I make my own values, maybe not consciously: and besides, who is "I"? For Byronic Romantics, "I" is indeed an individual, the outsider, the adventurer, the outlaw, he who defies society and accepted values, and follows his own—it may be to his doom, but this is better than conformity, enslavement to mediocrity. But for other thinkers "I" becomes something much more metaphysical. It is a collective—a nation, a Church, a Party, a class, an edifice in which I am only a stone, an organism of which I am only a tiny living fragment. *It* is the creator; I myself matter only insofar as I belong to the movement, the race, the nation, the class, the Church; I do not signify as a true individual within this super-person to whom my life is organically bound.

Hence German nationalism: I do this not because it is good or right or because I like it—I do it because I am a German and this is the German way to live. So also modern existentialism—I do it because I commit myself to this form of existence. Nothing makes me; I do not do it because it is an objective order which I obey, or because of universal rules to which I must adhere; I do it because I create my own life as I do; being what I am, I give it direction and I am responsible for it. Denial of universal values, this emphasis on being above all an element in, and loyal to, a super self, is a dangerous moment in European history, and has led to a great deal that has been destructive and sinister in modern times; this is where it begins, in the political ruminations and theories of the earliest German Romantics and their disciples in France and elsewhere.[6]

I never for a moment accepted the idea of these

---

6. The Romantics viewed their notion of self-moving centers of historical activity, thrusting forward on their own terms, as ultimately subjective. These were arbitrary entities—whether Byronic, somewhat satanic figures at war with society, or heroes who mold around themselves groups of followers (robbers, in the case of Schiller's play) or entire nations (Lycurgus, Moses—nation-builders so much admired by Machiavelli—to whom there are certainly modern parallels)—creating in accordance with freely invented patterns. This view was sternly

super-egos, but I recognized their importance in modern thought and action. Slogans like "Not I but the Party," "Not I but the Church," "My country right or wrong, but my country" have inflicted a wound on the central faith of human thought as I outlined it above—that the truth is universal, eternal, for all men at all times—from which it has never recovered. Mankind not as an object but as a subject, an ever-moving spirit, self-creating and self-moving, a self-composed drama in many acts, which, according to Marx, will end in some kind of perfection—all this issues from the Romantic revolution. While I reject this huge metaphysical interpretation of human life in

---

opposed by such thinkers as Hegel and Marx, who taught, each in his own fashion, that progress must conform to the iron laws of historical development—whether material development, as in Marx, or spiritual, as in Hegel. Only thus can the emancipation of human powers from irrational drives be achieved, and a reign be ushered in of total justice, freedom, virtue, happiness, and harmonious self-realization. This idea of inexorable progress is inherited from the Judeo-Christian tradition, but without the notions of the inscrutable divine will or the Last Judgment of mankind—the separation of the satisfactory sheep from the unsatisfactory goats—conducted after death.

49

toto—I remain an empiricist, and know only what I am able to experience, or think I could experience, and do not begin to believe in supra-individual entities—nevertheless I own that it made some impact on me, in the following way.

PLURALISM

I came to the conclusion that there is a plurality of ideals, as there is a plurality of cultures and of temperaments. I am not a relativist; I do not say "I like my coffee with milk and you like it without; I am in favor of kindness and you prefer concentration camps"—each of us with his own values, which cannot be overcome or integrated. This I believe to be false. But I do believe that there is a plurality of values which men can and do seek, and that these values differ. There is not an infinity of them: the number of human values, of values which I can pursue while maintaining my human semblance, my human character, is finite—let us say 74, or perhaps 122, or 26, but finite, whatever it may be. And the difference this makes is that if a man pursues one of these values, I, who do not, am able to understand why he pursues it or what it would be like, in his circumstances, for me to be induced to pursue it. Hence the possibility of human understanding.

I think these values are objective—that is to say, their nature, the pursuit of them, is part of what it is to be a human being, and this is an objective given. The fact that men are men and women are women and not dogs or cats or tables or chairs is an objective fact; and part of this objective fact is that there are certain values, and only those values, which men, while remaining men, can pursue. If I am a man or a woman with sufficient imagination (and this I do need), I can enter into a value system which is not my own, but which is nevertheless something I can conceive of men pursuing while remaining human, while remaining creatures with whom I can communicate, with whom I have some common values—for all human beings must have some common values or they cease to be human, and also some different values else they cease to differ, as in fact they do.

That is why pluralism is not relativism—the multiple values are objective, part of the essence of humanity rather than arbitrary creations of men's subjective fancies. Nevertheless, of course, if I pursue one set of values I may detest another, and may think it is damaging to the only form of life that I am able to live or tolerate, for myself and others; in which case I may attack it, I may even—in extreme cases—have to go to war against it. But I still recognize it as a human pursuit. I find Nazi values detestable, but I can understand how, given enough misinformation, enough false belief about reality, one could come to believe that they are the only salvation. Of course they have to be fought, by war if need be, but I do not regard the Nazis, as some people do, as literally pathological or insane, only as wickedly wrong, totally misguided about the facts, for example in believing that some beings are subhuman, or that race is central, or that Nordic races alone are truly creative, and so forth. I see how, with enough false education, enough widespread illusion and error, men can, while remaining men, believe this and commit the most unspeakable crimes.

If pluralism is a valid view, and respect between systems of values which are not necessarily hostile to each other is possible, then toleration and liberal consequences follow, as they do not either from monism (only one set of values is true, all the others are false) or from relativism (my values are mine, yours are yours, and if we clash, too bad, neither of us can claim to be right). My political pluralism is a product of reading Vico and Herder, and of understanding the roots of Romanticism, which in its violent, pathological form went too far for human toleration.

So with nationalism: the sense of belonging to a nation seems to me quite natural and not in itself to be condemned, or even criticized. But in its inflamed condition—my nation is better than yours, I know how the world should be shaped and you must yield because you do not, because you are inferior to me, because my nation is top and yours is far, far below mine and must offer itself as material to mine, which is the only nation entitled to create the best possible world—it is a form of pathological extremism which can lead, and has led, to unimaginable horrors, and is totally incompatible with the kind of pluralism which I have attempted to describe.

It may be of interest to remark, incidentally, that there are certain values that we in our world accept which were probably created by early Romanticism and did not exist before: for example, the idea that variety is a good thing, that a society in which many opinions are held, and those holding different opinions are tolerant of each other, is better than a monolithic society in which one opinion is binding on everyone. Nobody before the eighteenth century could have accepted that: the truth was one and the idea of variety was inimical to it. Again, the idea of sincerity, as a value, is something new. It was always right to be a martyr to the truth, but only to the truth: Muslims who died for Islam were poor, foolish, misled creatures who died for nonsense; so, for Catholics, were Protestants and Jews and pagans; and the fact that they held their beliefs sincerely made them no better—what was important was to be right. In discovering the truth, as in every other walk of life, success was what was important, not motive. If a man says to you that he believes that twice two is seventeen, and someone says, "You know, he doesn't do it to annoy you, he doesn't do it because he wants to show off or because he has been paid to say it—he truly believes, he is a sincere believer," you would say, "This makes it no better, he is talking irrational nonsense." That is what Protestants were doing, in the view of Catholics, and vice versa. The more sincere, the more dangerous; no marks were given for sincerity until the notion that there is more than one answer to a question—that is, pluralism—became more widespread. That is what led value to be set on motive rather than on consequence, on sincerity rather than on success.

The enemy of pluralism is monism—the ancient belief that there is a single harmony of truths into which everything, if it is genuine, in the end must fit. The consequence of this belief (which is something different from, but akin to, what Karl Popper called essentialism—to him the root of all evil) is that those who know should command those who do not. Those who know the answers to some of the great problems of mankind must be obeyed, for they alone know how society should be organized, how individual lives should be lived, how culture should be developed. This is the old Platonic belief in the philosopher-kings, who were entitled to give orders to others. There have always been thinkers who hold that if only scientists, or scientifically trained persons, could be put in charge of things, the world would be vastly improved. To this I have to say that no better excuse, or even reason, has ever been propounded for unlimited despotism on the part of an elite which robs the majority of its essential liberties.

Someone once remarked that in the old days men

and women were brought as sacrifices to a variety of gods; for these, the modern age has substituted new idols: isms. To cause pain, to kill, to torture are in general rightly condemned; but if these things are done not for my personal benefit but for an ism —socialism, nationalism, fascism, communism, fanatically held religious belief, or progress, or the fulfillment of the laws of history—then they are in order. Most revolutionaries believe, covertly or overtly, that in order to create the ideal world eggs must be broken, otherwise one cannot obtain the omelette. Eggs are certainly broken—never more violently or ubiquitously than in our times—but the omelette is far to seek, it recedes into an infinite distance. That is one of the corollaries of unbridled monism, as I call it—some call it fanaticism, but monism is at the root of every extremism.

FREEDOM

Political freedom is a topic to which I devoted two lectures during the 1950s. The later of these, entitled "Two Concepts of Liberty,"[7] inaugurated my Oxford Professorship, and its gist was to distinguish between two notions of liberty (or freedom—the terms are used interchangeably), negative and positive. By negative liberty I meant the absence of obstacles which block human action. Quite apart from obstacles created by the external world, or by the biological, physiological, psychological laws which govern human beings, there is lack of political freedom—the central topic of my lecture —where the obstacles are man-made, whether deliberately or unintentionally. The extent of negative liberty depends on the degree to which such man-made obstacles are absent—on the degree to

---

7. Delivered in 1958, and available in two collections of essays by the author: *Four Essays on Liberty* (Oxford University Press, 1969) and *The Proper Study of Mankind: An Anthology of Essays* (Farrar, Straus and Giroux, 1998).

which I am free to go down this or that path without being prevented from doing so by man-made institutions or disciplines, or by the activities of specific human beings.

It is not enough to say that negative freedom simply means freedom to do what I like, for in that case I can liberate myself from obstacles to the fulfillment of desire simply by following the ancient Stoics and killing desire. But that path, the gradual elimination of the desires to which obstacles can occur, leads in the end to humans being gradually deprived of their natural, living activities: in other words, the most perfectly free human beings will be those who are dead, since then there is no desire and therefore no obstacles. What I had in mind, rather, was simply the number of paths down which a man can walk, whether or not he chooses to do so. That is the first of the two basic senses of political freedom.

Some have maintained, against me, that freedom must be a triadic relationship: I can overcome or remove or be free from obstacles only in order to do something, to be free to perform a given act or acts.

But I do not accept that. Unfreedom in its basic sense is what we ascribe to the man in jail, or the man tied to a tree; all that such a man seeks is the breaking of his chains, escape from the cell, without necessarily aiming at a particular activity once he is liberated. In the larger sense, of course, freedom means freedom from the rules of a society or its institutions, from the deployment against one of excessive moral or physical force, or from whatever shuts off possibilities of action which otherwise would be open. This I call "freedom from."

The other central sense of freedom is freedom *to*: if my negative freedom is specified by answering the question "How far am I controlled?" the question for the second sense of freedom is "Who controls me?" Since we are talking about man-made obstacles, I can ask myself "Who determines my actions, my life? Do I do so, freely, in whatever way I choose? Or am I under orders from some other source of control? Is my activity determined by parents, schoolmasters, priests, policemen? Am I under the discipline of a legal system, the capitalist order, a slaveowner, the government (monarchical, oligarchic, democratic)? In what sense am I master of my fate? My possibilities of action may be limited, but how are they limited? Who are those who stand in my way, how much power can they wield?"

These are the two central senses of "liberty" which I set myself to investigate. I realized that they differed, that they were answers to two different questions; but, although cognate, they did not in my view clash—the answer to one did not necessarily determine the answer to the other. Both freedoms were ultimate human ends, both were necessarily limited, and both concepts could be perverted in the course of human history. Negative liberty could be interpreted as economic laissez faire, whereby in the name of freedom owners are allowed to destroy the lives of children in mines, or factory owners to destroy the health and character of workers in industry. But that was a perversion, not what the concept basically means to human beings, in my view. Equally it was said that it is a mockery to inform a poor man that he is perfectly free to occupy a room in an expensive hotel, although he may not be able to pay for it. But that, too, is a confusion. He is indeed free to rent a room there, but has not the means of using this freedom. He has not the means, perhaps, because he has been prevented from earning more than he does by a man-made economic system—but that is a deprivation of freedom to earn money, not of freedom to rent the room. This may sound a pedantic distinction, but it is central to discussions of economic versus political freedom.

The notion of positive freedom has led, historically, to even more frightful perversions. Who orders my life? I do. I? Ignorant, confused, driven hither and thither by uncontrolled passions and drives—is that all there is to me? Is there not within me a higher, more rational, freer self, able to understand and dominate passions, ignorance, and other defects, which I can attain to only by a process of education or understanding, a process which can be managed only by those who are wiser than myself, who make me aware of my true, "real," deepest self, of what I am at my best? This is a well-known metaphysical view, according to which I can be truly free and self-controlled only if I am truly rational—a belief which goes back to Plato—and since I am not perhaps sufficiently rational myself, I must obey those who are indeed rational, and who therefore know what is best not only for themselves but also for me, and who can guide me along lines which will ultimately awaken my true rational self and put it in charge, where it truly belongs. I may feel hemmed in—indeed, crushed—by these authorities, but that is an illusion: when I have grown up and have attained to a fully mature, "real" self, I shall understand that I would have done for myself what has been done for me if I had been as wise, when I was in an inferior condition, as they are now.

In short, they are acting on my behalf, in the interests of my higher self, in controlling my lower self; so that true liberty for the lower self consists in total obedience to them, the wise, those who know the truth, the elite of sages; or perhaps my obedience must be to those who understand how human destiny is made—for if Marx is right, then it is a Party (which alone grasps the demands of the rational goals of history) which must shape and guide me, whichever way my poor empirical self may wish to go; and the Party itself must be guided by its far-seeing leaders, and in the end by the greatest and wisest leader of all.

There is no despot in the world who cannot use this method of argument for the vilest oppression, in the name of an ideal self which he is seeking to bring to fruition by his own, perhaps somewhat brutal and *prima facie* morally odious means (*prima facie* only for the lower empirical self). The "engineer of human souls," to use Stalin's phrase,[8] knows best; he does what he does not simply in

---

8. Stalin used the phrase "engineers of human souls" in a speech on the role of Soviet writers made at Maxim Gorky's house on October 26, 1932, recorded in an unpublished manuscript in the Gorky archive—K. L. Zelinsky, "Vstrecha pisatelei s I. V. Stalinym" ("A meeting of writers with I. V. Stalin")—and published for the first time, in English, in A. Kemp-Welch, *Stalin and the Literary Intelligentsia, 1928–39* (Macmillan [UK], 1991), pp. 128–131: for this phrase see p. 131 (and, for the

order to do his best for his nation, but in the name of the nation itself, in the name of what the nation would be doing itself if only it had attained to this level of historical understanding. That is the great perversion which the positive notion of liberty has been liable to: whether the tyranny issues from a Marxist leader, a king, a fascist dictator, the masters of an authoritarian Church or class or State, it seeks for the imprisoned, "real" self within men, and "liberates" it, so that this self can attain to the level of those who give the orders.

This goes back to the naive notion that there is only one true answer to every question: if I know the true answer and you do not, and you disagree with me, it is because you are ignorant; if you knew the truth, you would necessarily believe what I believe; if you seek to disobey me, this can be so only because you are wrong, because the truth has not been revealed to you as it has been to me. This

---

Russian original, "inzhenery chelovecheskikh dush," I. V. Stalin, *Sochineniya* (Moscow, 1946–1967), Vol. 13, p. 410).—*H. H.*

justifies some of the most frightful forms of oppression and enslavement in human history, and it is truly the most dangerous, and, in our century in particular, the most violent, interpretation of the notion of positive liberty.

This notion of two kinds of liberty and their distortions then formed the center of much discussion and dispute in Western and other universities, and does so to this day.

DETERMINISM

My other lecture on freedom was entitled "Historical Inevitability."[9] Here I stated that determinism was a doctrine very widely accepted among philosophers for many hundreds of years. Determinism declares that every event has a cause, from

9. Delivered in 1953, and also included both in *Four Essays on Liberty* and in *The Proper Study of Mankind*.

which it unavoidably follows. This is the foundation of the natural sciences: the laws of nature and all their applications—the entire body of natural science—rest upon the notion of an eternal order which the sciences investigate. But if the rest of nature is subject to these laws, can it be that man alone is not? When a man supposes, as most ordinary people do (though not most scientists and philosophers), that when he rises from the chair he need not have done so, that he did so because he chose to do so, but he need not have chosen—when he supposes this, he is told that this is an illusion, that even though the necessary work by psychologists has not yet been accomplished, one day it will be (or at any rate in principle can be), and then he will know that what he is and does is necessarily as it is, and could not be otherwise. I believe this doctrine to be false, but I do not in this essay seek to demonstrate this, or to refute determinism— indeed, I am not sure if such a demonstration or refutation is possible. My only concern is to ask myself two questions. Why do philosophers and others think that human beings are fully determined? And, if they are, is this compatible with normal moral sentiments and behavior, as commonly understood?

My thesis is that there are two main reasons for supporting the doctrine of human determinism. The first is that, since the natural sciences are perhaps the greatest success story in the whole history of mankind, it seems absurd to suppose that man alone is not subject to the natural laws discovered by the scientists. (That, indeed, is what the eighteenth-century *philosophes* maintained.) The question is not, of course, whether man is wholly free of such laws—no one but a madman could maintain that man does not depend on his biological or psychological structure or environment, or on the laws of nature. The only question is: Is his liberty totally exhausted thereby? Is there not some corner in which he can act as he chooses, and not be determined to choose by antecedent causes? This may be a tiny corner of the realm of nature, but unless it is there, his consciousness of being free, which is undoubtedly all but universal—the fact that most people believe that, while some of their actions are mechanical, some obey their free will—is an enormous illusion, from the beginnings of mankind, ever since Adam ate the apple, although told not to do so, and did not reply, "I could not help it, I did not do it freely, Eve forced me to do it."

The second reason for belief in determinism is that it does devolve the responsibility for a great many things that people do on to impersonal causes, and therefore leaves them in a sense unblameworthy for what they do. When I make a mistake, or commit a wrong or a crime, or do anything else which I recognize, or which others recognize, as bad or unfortunate, I can say, "How could I avoid it?—that was the way I was brought up" or "That is my nature, something for which natural laws are responsible" or "I belong to a society, a class, a Church, a nation, in which everyone does it, and nobody seems to condemn it" or "I am psychologically conditioned by the way in which my parents behaved to each other and to me, and by the economic and social circumstances in which I was placed, or was forced into, not to be able to choose to act otherwise" or, finally, "I was under orders."

Against this, most people believe that everyone has at least two choices that he can make, two possibilities that he can realize. When Eichmann says, "I killed Jews because I was ordered to; if I had not done it I would have been killed myself," one can say, "I see that it is improbable that you would have chosen to be killed, but in principle you could have done it if you had decided to do it—there was no literal compulsion, as there is in nature, that caused you to act as you did." You may say it is unreasonable to expect people to behave like that when facing great dangers: so it is, but however unlikely it may be that they should decide to do so, in the literal sense of the word they *could* have chosen to do so. Martyrdom cannot be expected, but can be accepted, against whatever odds—indeed, that is why it is so greatly admired.

So much for the reasons for which men choose to embrace determinism in history. But if they do, there is a difficult logical consequence, to say the least. It means that we cannot say to anyone, "Did you have to do that? Why need you have done that?"—the assumption behind which is that he could have refrained, or done something else. The whole of our common morality, in which we speak of obligation and duty, right and wrong, moral praise and blame—the way in which people are praised or condemned, rewarded or punished, for behaving in a way in which they were not forced to behave, when they could have behaved otherwise—this network of beliefs and practices, on which all current morality seems to me to depend, presupposes the notion of responsibility, and responsibility entails the ability to choose between black and white, right and wrong, pleasure and duty; as well as, in a wider sense, between forms of life, forms of government, and the whole constellations of moral values in terms of which most people, however much they may or may not be aware of it, do in fact live.

If determinism were accepted, our vocabulary

would have to be very, very radically changed. I do not say that this is impossible in principle, but it goes further than what most people are prepared to face. At best, aesthetics would have to replace morality. You can admire or praise people for being handsome, or generous, or musical—but that is not a matter of their choice, that is "how they are made." Moral praise would have to take the same form: if I praise you for saving my life at your own risk, I mean that it is wonderful that you are so made that you could not avoid doing this, and I am glad that I encountered someone literally determined to save my life, as opposed to someone else who was determined to look the other way. Honorable or dishonorable conduct, pleasure-seeking and heroic martyrdom, courage and cowardice, deceitfulness and truthfulness, doing right against temptation—these would become like being good-looking or ugly, tall or short, old or young, black or white, born of English or Italian parents: something that we cannot alter, for everything is determined. We can hope that things will go as we should like, but we cannot do anything toward this—we are so made that we cannot help but act in a particular fashion. Indeed, the very notion of an act denotes choice; but if choice is itself determined, what is the difference between action and mere behavior?

It seems to me paradoxical that some political movements demand sacrifices and yet are determinist in belief. Marxism, for example, which is founded on historical determinism—the inevitable stages through which society must pass before it reaches perfection—enjoins painful and dangerous acts, coercion and killing, equally painful at times both to the perpetrators and to the victims; but if history will inevitably bring about the perfect society, why should one sacrifice one's life for a process which will, without one's help, reach its proper, happy destination? Yet there is a curious human feeling that if the stars in their courses are fighting for you, so that your cause will triumph, then you should sacrifice yourself in order to shorten the process, to bring the birth-pangs of the new order nearer, as Marx said. But can so many people be truly persuaded to face these dangers, just to shorten a process which will end in happiness whatever they may do or fail to do? This has always puzzled me, and puzzled others.

All this I discussed in the lecture in question, which has remained controversial, and has been much discussed and disputed, and is so still.

THE PURSUIT OF THE IDEAL

There is one further topic which I have written about, and that is the very notion of a perfect society, the solution to all our ills. Some of the eighteenth-century French *philosophes* thought the ideal society they hoped for would inevitably come; others were more pessimistic and supposed that human defects would fail to bring it about. Some thought that progress toward it was inexorable, others that only great human effort could achieve it, but might not do so. However this may be, the very notion of the ideal society presupposes the conception of a perfect world in which all the great values in the light of which men have lived for so long can be realized together, at least in principle. Quite apart from the fact that the idea had seemed Utopian to those who thought that such a world could not be achieved because of material or psychological obstacles, or the incurable ignorance, weakness, or lack of rationality of men, there is a far more formidable objection to the very notion itself.

I do not know who else may have thought this, but it occurred to me that some ultimate values are compatible with each other and some are not. Liberty, in whichever sense, is an eternal human ideal, whether individual or social. So is equality. But perfect liberty (as it must be in the perfect world) is not compatible with perfect equality. If man is free to do anything he chooses, then the strong will crush the weak, the wolves will eat the sheep, and this puts an end to equality. If perfect equality is to be attained, then men must be prevented from outdistancing each other, whether in material or in intellectual or in spiritual achievement, otherwise inequalities will result. The anarchist Bakunin, who believed in equality above all, thought that universities should be abolished because they bred learned men who behaved as if they were superior to the unlearned, and this propped up social inequalities. Similarly, a world of perfect justice—and who can deny that this is one of the noblest of human values?—is not compatible with perfect mercy. I need not labor this point: either the law takes its toll, or men forgive, but the two values cannot both be realized.

Again, knowledge and happiness may or may not be compatible. Rationalist thinkers have supposed that knowledge always liberates, that it saves men from being victims of forces they cannot understand; to some degree this is no doubt true, but if I know that I have cancer I am not thereby made happier, or freer—I must choose between always knowing as much as I can and accepting that there are situations where ignorance may be bliss. Nothing is more attractive than spontaneous creativity, natural vitality, a free flowering of ideas, works of art—but these are not often compatible with a capacity for careful and effective planning, without which no even moderately secure society can be created.

Liberty and equality, spontaneity and security, happiness and knowledge, mercy and justice—all these are ultimate human values, sought for themselves alone; yet when they are incompatible, they cannot all be attained, choices must be made, sometimes tragic losses accepted in the pursuit of some preferred ultimate end. But if, as I believe, this is not merely empirically but conceptually true—that is, derives from the very conception of these values—then the very idea of the perfect world in which all good things are realized is incomprehensible, is in fact conceptually incoherent. And if this is so, and I cannot see how it could be otherwise, then the very notion of the ideal world, for which no sacrifice can be too great, vanishes from view.

To go back to the Encyclopedists and the
Marxists and all the other movements the purpose
of which is the perfect life: it seems as if the doctrine
that all kinds of monstrous cruelties must be permitted, because without these the ideal state of
affairs cannot be attained—all the justifications of
broken eggs for the sake of the ultimate omelette,
all the brutalities, sacrifices, brainwashing, all those
revolutions, everything that has made this century
perhaps the most appalling of any since the days of
old, at any rate in the West—all this is for nothing,
for the perfect universe is not merely unattainable
but inconceivable, and everything done to bring
it about is founded on an enormous intellectual
fallacy.

TRIBUTES TO

ISAIAH BERLIN

Noel
Annan

- - - - -

The following address

was delivered

at a Memorial Service

at the Hampstead Synagogue

on January 14, 1998

WHEN I HEARD that Isaiah Berlin had died, I sat down and read the letters we had written each other since 1950, and he lived again. He wrote as he talked, and he was the most dazzling talker of his generation. Strangers might hardly understand a word because his tongue had to sprint to keep up with the pace of his thoughts. Ideas, similes, metaphors cascaded over each other. His talk was sustained by a fabulous memory for names, events, and the motives of the participants in his stories. It was like watching a pageant. As Dr. Johnson said of Richard Savage, "at no time in his life was it any part of his character to be the first of the company that desired to separate." At New College and All Souls he talked until his exhausted guest tottered to bed, only to find Berlin sitting on the end of it, unwilling to bring the evening to an end. On the historic occasion when he called on Anna Akhmatova they talked straight through the night.

No one else was remotely like him. Of course he had charm, but he had more than that. He was a Magus, a magician when he spoke, and it was for his character and personality as much as for his published works that so many honors fell upon him. The *Evening Standard* spoke truth when it said, "The respectful sadness that met his death and the enormous regard in which he was held shows that intellectuals can still be prized as civilising influences in Britain." He was loved by people with whom he had nothing in common—millionaires, obscure writers, world-famous musicians, public figures, and young unknown scholars to whom he listened. Whatever the circle, he civilized it; and the world is a little less civilized now that he has left it.

Generosity came naturally to him. He was never sneaky or malevolent as a critic. Indeed he tried too hard, perhaps, to avoid giving offense. "I enjoy being able to praise," he said. He never intrigued to meet the geniuses of his time—Freud, Einstein, Virginia Woolf, Russell, Pasternak, Stravinsky—and he had no shame in admitting that he was greatly excited when he did meet them. His oldest friends, Stuart Hampshire or Stephen Spender, were especially dear to him. Yet he had an eye for human failings and noted feet of clay, even of people he esteemed. He did not censure, but he did not condone ungentle behavior or sexual exhibitionism. "I feel acutely uncomfortable," he wrote me, "in the presence of Beaverbrook, Cherwell, Radcliffe or Driberg." People who rejected equality as a goal were deeply unsympathetic to him. Equality had to give way often to liberty, but so did liberty sometimes to equality. For instance, he thought that the price England paid for the public schools was too high.

Nicolas Nabokov accused him of liking bores too much. But then Isaiah was meticulous in obeying the obligations of a scholar. No one was ever turned away who came to him genuinely wishing to discuss a problem. To watch him at Mishkenot Sha'ananim in Jerusalem, spending hours with those who queued to seek his advice, was to realize that he honored anyone in search of truth. Those who have never believed, he wrote of the days when the young Oxford philosophers met with Austin and Ayer, that they were discovering for the first time some new truth that might have profound influence upon philosophy, "those who have never been under the spell of this kind of illusion, even for a short while, have not known true intellectual happiness."

Very few people are able to write unforgettably about liberty. Rousseau did; John Stuart Mill did; and in our own times, Schumpeter and E. M. Forster did. But, as Forster once said of himself in a parody of Landor: "I warmed both hands before the fire of life, And put it out." Isaiah made it blaze. He took the unfashionable view that liberty meant not being impeded by others. He distrusted Rousseau's and Hegel's theory of positive freedom as a perversion of common sense. To deny free will—to believe in the inevitability of an historical process—to portray man as imprisoned by the impersonal forces of history—that ran against our deepest experience. He believed the creation of the state of Israel proved that history is not predetermined. Israel owed its existence to Weizmann, yet all Weizmann's schemes were swept away by fortuitous events. And what could be less inevitable than the survival of Britain in 1940? To Berlin, the very methods that Marxists, economists, and sociologists used prevented them from discovering what is at the heart of men and women. He distrusted technocrats in government and sapient Reports with their self-confident proposals for restructuring institutions. That was why he did not pontificate on daily issues. Monetarism, social security schemes, were not for him. He disappointed President Kennedy by not advancing views on the number needed of ICBMs.

But there was one public issue on which he left no one in doubt. Above all, Isaiah was a Jew, and never forgave those who forgot to conceal their anti-Semitism, the nastier ways of snubs, pinpricks, acts of exclusion, which we Gentiles inflict upon Jews, and in so doing defile ourselves. He was a Zionist precisely because he felt that however well Jews were treated and accepted by the country they lived in, they felt uneasy and insecure. That was why they needed a country of their own where Jews could live like other nations. As he lay dying, he declared that the partition of the Holy Land was the only solution to give Palestinians rights to their land and give Israel Jerusalem as its capital city with the Muslim holy places under a Muslim authority, and an Arab quarter under UN protection. He never felt the smallest difficulty in being loyal to Judah and loyal to Britain. When he worked during the war in Washington, he told American Zionists that he was the servant of the British government—but its servant, not its conscript. At any time, he could resign if he decided British policy was unforgivable. He was proud to belong to Britain, to that country which Weizmann had praised for its moderation, dislike of extremes, a humane democracy.

There was another claimant for his loyalty—
Oxford. He thought he owed it a debt. He paid
that debt when, against the advice of his most
intimate friends, he agreed to become head of a
new Oxford college. Who can doubt that it was
Isaiah's personality that convinced Mac Bundy of
the Ford Foundation and Isaac and Leonard
Wolfson, renowned for their princely generosity,
to build and endow a new college with Isaiah
as President? President, not Master. The Master of
Wolfson sounded to Isaiah too much like a Scottish
laird, and he did not fancy himself in a kilt. Many
of the chores he left to the faithful Michael Brock;
but it was Isaiah who negotiated the deal with the
University and strangled some dingy proposals for
shackling the new place. And it was Isaiah who
travelled 4,000 miles to interview architects, select
materials, and convince the sixty Fellows with
barely a dissenting voice.

He was a man of invincible modesty. But for
Henry Hardy we would never have had his col-
lected works. He genuinely believed that he was

overrated and deserved few of the honors he was given. "I have a pathological dislike of personal publicity," he wrote me. "It is like a terror of bats or spiders. I am not a public figure like A. J. P. Taylor, Graham Greene, Arthur Schlesinger, or Kenneth Clark. Nor an ideologue like Tawney, Cole, Oakeshott. Perhaps not as bad as Crossman and a good many others thought me to be, a well-disposed amiable rattle." For years he had no entry in *Who's Who*, until he found the entry form he had left lying about had been filled in by Maurice Bowra, with scandalous fictitious achievements. Then he gave in.

To have lived without music would have been to him a nightmare. Unthinkable to live without Bach, unendurable without Beethoven and Schubert. He loved Verdi for the uninhibited tunes and for Verdi's hatred of aristocratic brutality and tyranny. No one, he thought, had ever played the Beethoven posthumous quartets like the Busch ensemble. He admitted that Toscanini was not the man for the thick brew of Wagner; but when one saw Toscanini as well as heard him the authority was such that, so he wrote me, "this and this only was the truth—the intensity, the seriousness and the sublime *terribilità* totally subdued you." Walter, Klemperer and Mahler and the luxuriant valleys of Furtwängler, yes—but Toscanini was Everest—compared with him he said the rest were not fit to tie his shoelaces, mere Apennines covered with villas. Yet in his later years he found a friend, an intellectual as well as a profound musician, in Alfred Brendel; and he and his old friend Isaac Stern have honored him today.

He was at his happiest in a small group of intimate friends in Oxford colleges or sitting in a corner of the Russian Tea Room on 57th Street a few blocks down from the offices of *The New York Review of Books* with Robert Silvers, Stuart Hampshire, and the Lowells. In Oxford as a bachelor—in the days before the war he was always called Shaya, renowned as the most amusing young don in Oxford—in those days his door was always open. Colleagues, pupils, friends from

London dropped in to gossip. He loved gossip. An election to a chair in Oxford or Cambridge would inspire him to give a dramatic performance of the proceedings. The treachery of Bloggs, the craven behavior of Stiggins, the twitterings of the outside electors, and when it came to the vote, the *volte-face*, the defection of those you had imagined were your closest allies. Brought up to imagine that such proceedings were sacred and secret, priggish Cambridge visitors such as myself reeled.

What made those excursions into fantasy all the more enchanting was Isaiah's irrepressible sense of humor. It was not English humor. It came from the Russian part of his makeup; from Gogol, from Chekhov. He loved jokes. He loved games. Who was a hedgehog, who was a fox? What is the difference between a cad and a bounder? When others were maddened by the perverse, egoistic, self-satisfied speeches in a college meeting, Isaiah revelled in them—to him they revealed the perennial eccentricity of human beings. Let none of us, however, be deceived. The lot of human beings, he saw, was tragic. And why? They are made of crooked timber.

As the years pass, bachelor life in college becomes exhausting, and in 1956 the greatest stroke of good fortune that ever befell him occurred. He married Aline. She transformed his life without changing it—if the contradiction be permitted. She gave him what he had always needed: love. As solicitous as she was beautiful, she caressed his existence in Albany, in Portofino, and in Headington. Like him, she disliked ostentation. Aline had been a great competitor when she was golf champion of France, but she never competed with Isaiah. She was there as the setting in which he shone—perpetually anxious that all should go well for him, not for her. She brought him a family, her children Michel Strauss, Peter and Philippe Halban, and her young Gunzbourg cousins, for whom he was a new uncle. To the delight of Isaiah's friends, they created a new persona, calling him "Ton-ton Isaïe."

And now he is gone. If I have not spoken

sufficiently of his defense of liberty or pluralism, or of his detestation of cruelty and ruthlessness, it is because I speak of him as a friend. Political thinkers and intellectuals, so I believe, have not yet understood how disquieting is his contention that good ends conflict. Isaiah Berlin was original, and he is as hard to come to terms with as Machiavelli or Hume. All I can say is that he seems to me to have offered the truest and most moving interpretation of life that my own generation made.

And I must add this. I owe everything to my teachers. They taught me to learn and, if I got above myself, how much more I had to learn. I was never, of course, one of Isaiah's students, but I never failed to learn from him. He taught me to think more clearly, to feel more deeply, to hope, and to put my trust in life.

NOEL ANNAN

Stuart Hampshire

- - - - -

The following address

was delivered at the

Commemoration in the

Sheldonian Theatre, Oxford,

on March 21, 1998

I SHALL ATTEMPT a personal and intellectual remembrance of Isaiah Berlin from 1935 onward. In 1935 in Llandudno, North Wales, in Boots' Circulating Library, I came across Kafka's *Great Wall of China and Other Stories*, just translated by Edwin and Willa Muir, and I was overwhelmed. Isaiah had mentioned Kafka in the magazine *Oxford Outlook*, which he had co-edited with Dick Crossman. An undergraduate friend, Benedict Nicolson, introduced us so that we could talk about Kafka.

After that we persisted in talking, more or less continuously for sixty-two years, except for four war years, when Isaiah was in America. We gradually, in those pre-war years in All Souls, formed

97

the habit of discussing anything interesting that either of us experienced and of checking up on any changes in our opinions and in our loyalties, right up until the last week of his life. In the Thirties there existed among politicians, writers, intellectuals, in Britain and in Europe, a culture of paranoia, a feeling of being haunted by a specter of catastrophe, of a final settling of accounts that was to come. Kafka had diagnosed this mood of anxiety very exactly. But Isaiah, in his room in the Hawksmoor tower of All Souls, with his old-fashioned HMV gramophone with its immense horn for better sound, sharpening his fiber needles, playing the overture to Rossini's *La Scala di Seta* or *La Gazza Ladra*, or Schnabel's Beethoven or the Busch Quartet, Isaiah certainly did not share this sad fear of the world, whether the Marxist forms of fear, or the Freudian forms, or in the subtle form of philosophical skepticism. It soon emerged that he loved England, Oxford University, Salzburg, Italy, the London Library, and All Souls College. He was boundlessly benevolent, approachable, gentle, constantly telling stories, and sweeping one along with them. In his All Souls rooms he kept over the mantelpiece a painting, the work of an undergraduate friend, Giles Robertson, which showed him as a small child dangerously perched on a windowsill over the street. Far away from Riga he was utterly at home in pre-war Oxford, happily involved in College affairs and with devoted pupils. In his thought he was at that time, and he remained, a convinced and calm empiricist, who insisted that the stuff of our day-to-day experience, whether in personal experience or in politics, is the true stuff of reality, and that behind the phases of history there lurks no hidden plot either of punishment or of redemption. He took the furniture of the world, both the natural and the social furniture, medium-sized objects on a human scale, to be entirely real and to exist more or less as we perceive them. The Nazis, steadily advancing toward us in those years, were just a manifest and unmitigated evil, and the evil was not for him a sign of something beyond itself, needing to be interpreted, but simply a hideous reality to be resisted. The appeasers, both of the Left and the Right, with their different theories of history, were for him just wrong, wrong through ignoring natural feelings.

Apart from the Nazis and Zionism and Socialism, we talked, for much of the time, about the new analytical philosophy. Typically, it was in Isaiah's room that a group of younger philosophers met on Thursday evenings during term. He was the co-ordinating, animating center. He always resisted the schematization of language, and of the sources of knowledge, which logical positivism required. He was always a pluralist in epistemology as later in the theory of politics and of morality. At least two of his journal articles, strikingly original in their time, are still important half a century later. There was no great discontinuity when after the war he turned away from academic philosophy to the history of ideas. To reconstruct and to reanimate the images and fantasies that lay behind the arguments of abstract thinkers was a constant passion of his, and in lectures on Russian thinkers and on

the Enlightenment and the Counter-Enlightenment,
both in Oxford and on the BBC, he created his own
public. I remember standing with him on the lawn
at All Souls reading some of the letters, unprece-
dented in number, which the BBC had received from
listeners who had been fascinated by the very various personalities he had conjured up for them in his
headlong style. This response to his lectures was
repeated in universities all over America as well as
in Oxford. Like William James, whom he greatly
admired, his thought was naturally rhetorical and
declamatory, and he liked to let himself go in his
eulogies, and particularly in celebrating the oddities
and insights of unconforming minds. He enjoyed
those cascades of proper names which I am sure all
who heard his lectures will remember: the names
were the lights from the other shore that he felt
should always be kept alight.

Finally, I must come to the person, to the man of
feeling, in one sense of that phrase, which I think
was his essence. He responded immediately to tones
of voice, to the quality and to the intention of a

person's smile, and to the lilt of his or her sentences, and to the displays and disguises of a conversation and of a personality. In speech he could make himself become David Cecil or Henry Price or Maurice Bowra, three friends among many whom he was delighted to impersonate. But his life was reconstituted, started all over again, when he married Aline in 1956. He effectively had two lives enclosed in one, pre-Aline and then with her, and the second life, in its wholeness and completeness, realized for him an undreamt-of happiness. Because of his unalterable modesty, he was surprised by his destiny, just as he was later surprised by the accumulation of honors and titles and prizes, and by the fame and acclamation of all sorts, that came to him in these later years. I can speak here, among his friends, about the uncounted trails of affectionate memory in so many directions that he left behind, in London, Jerusalem, Washington, and elsewhere, the many people who enjoyed the sense of having some special intimacy with him, in some cases, an intimacy as with no one else. How did this come about? What was the peculiar quality that explains this multiplication of friendships, quite apart from his evident brilliance and virtuosity and the astonishing range of his knowledge?

One feature of his character which greatly contributed, I believe, was his deep-seated unvarying patience—patience in attending to people, in constantly thinking about them, and about their needs. For example, from the pre-war years onward he was a kind of consul general to foreign scholars visiting Oxford for the first time, who steadily over the years, and even before the war, found their way to his rooms in All Souls and later also to Headington House. This generous quality of his in giving time to people was connected with a complete absence of self-importance. He always refused to divide his time into measured bits and then to allocate it appropriately. This same habit of unhurriedness caused him to reject philosophies and theories that are in a hurry to explain, right now, the relation of the mind to the body or the movements of history, problems that probably still require a century or two of continuous thought, at the very least. Lastly he was tirelessly patient in overcoming the many obstacles to the foundation of Wolfson College, a project that was originally conceived as a kind of thank-offering to Britain when he was visiting Princeton. This was perhaps the greatest of all his many achievements. Finding first the endowment, then the site and the architect, winning the support of the university and also of the colleges, not easily but step by step—he seemed to possess the worldly skills and flair of a medieval Archbishop, of an Archbishop Chichele. The completed Wolfson vividly reflects in its structures and in its customs the unstuffy personality of its founder and its first president.

I therefore celebrate with you the very happy and the immensely constructive life of an extraordinary person, an extraordinary human being: and I mourn also a particular friend, an almost lifelong, and life-creating, friend.

STUART HAMPSHIRE

Avishai Margalit

- - - - -

The following address

was delivered at the

Commemoration in the

Sheldonian Theatre, Oxford,

on March 21, 1998

"YOU HAVE BEAUTIFUL black eyes," Greta Garbo once said to Isaiah Berlin. His eyes were indeed remarkably expressive. They were full of mischievous cleverness, childish inquisitiveness, and skeptical soberness. Today these eyes appear in framed photographs: glassy and formal. The spark is gone.

In recent years the conversations between us turned more frequently to the loss of the spark—to death. In one letter he asks: Do you think about death? In my situation, he writes, I naturally find myself thinking about it. He goes on to say, I believe in what Epicurus said: "Where I am, death is not, and where death is, I am not." I am not afraid of death, he used to say, but "what a waste!" This mention of Epicurus was not accidental. Isaiah believed the name Epicurus to be the source of the word *Apikores*, the traditional Jewish label for one who doubts the afterlife, divine revelation, and the authority of the rabbis. A skeptic, not a heretic.

One streak in Judaism which Isaiah was definitely very skeptical about is the idea that we are not here to enjoy ourselves. Isaiah enjoyed his life thoroughly, and made it his business to make others joyous in his presence. This business, of making others joyous, had its price. Or so Isaiah thought.

Every year, the *Frankfurter Allgemeine Zeitung* asks famous people questions like "Who would you like to have been?" Isaiah's answer: Alexander Herzen. To the question "Mention a flaw in your character," Isaiah replied, "Anxiousness to please." This was not a coy confession about a cute character flaw, designed to extract denials, or to fish for double compliments. I want to talk about what Isaiah regarded as a flaw in his character, because I believe that it relates to an issue of importance in Isaiah's life: it relates to his concern with fellow Jews and to his Zionism.

There's a wonderful lecture of Berlin's entitled "Jewish Slavery and Emancipation." In it, he spells out a parable for the state of the Jews which is eminently pertinent. He tells there of "travellers who by some accident find themselves among a tribe with whose customs they are not familiar." They don't know what to expect. "The strangers . . . being alien to this mode of life, find little they can take for granted." They "do everything they can to find out how their hosts 'function.' They must get this right, otherwise they may easily find themselves in trouble. . . . But then this is precisely the reason for which they are felt to be outsiders . . . they are experts on the tribe, not members of it." "They are," Berlin added, "altogether too anxious to please."

For Berlin, as for Tolstoy, the distinction between being natural and being artificial and affected is basic. Natasha in love, stung by a nettle in the field, is for Tolstoy an epiphany of the natural, while Natasha watching French opera, with a stage setting of a phony moon, is an emblem of the artificial. Isaiah, the avid opera worshiper, never considered the opera as artificial. He tied his own sense of the natural and the artificial with Friedrich Schiller's distinction, which was most meaningful to him, between the naive and the sentimental. The natural that is the naive is the one who is not conscious of any rift between oneself and one's surrounding, and who is not conscious of any rift within oneself. The artificial that is the sentimental is the one who is being painfully conscious of such rifts. Being at home for Isaiah meant the possibility of being natural, naive, and socially at ease. The Jews lost the sense of home by being in exile.

If anyone was at home in Oxford, Isaiah Berlin was the one. He was immensely grateful to English society for accepting him. Yet he sensed that due to his experience as an immigrant Jewish child he retained the anxiousness to please. This gave him, the great Versteher, the key for his imaginative leap for understanding what it is like to lack home. Zionism, for Isaiah, had one supreme goal: to endow the Jews with a sense of home. "Home," Isaiah liked to quote Robert Frost, "is the place where, when you have to go there, they have to take you in." This is how Isaiah saw the notion of a National Home for the Jews in the land of Israel. In spite of his criticism of Zionist politics, when it unnecessarily deprives Palestinian Arabs of their homes, he saw Zionism as a success story with regard to his central concern, the revival for the Jews of the sense of home.

Of the three sides of the revolutionary triangle—liberty, equality, and fraternity—Isaiah is known most for siding with liberty. But I believe that no less at the center of Isaiah's thought and feelings was the idea of fraternity, or human solidarity. He felt a basic, unapologetic solidarity with Jews everywhere. And this made him think about solidarity in general. For Berlin the Jews were not the carriers of a philosophy called Judaism. Isaiah never believed in the religious idea of the Jews as the chosen people, nor in secular versions of this idea. He believed even less in the idea that the long history of oppression and torment of the Jews attests to their being chosen. There was for him nothing sublime or redemptive in suffering. Suffering is suffering is suffering.

Once he put me to the test. That is—he tested me with a thought experiment. Suppose, he said, that you have at your disposal an Aladdin's lamp. When you rub it, miraculous things happen. You can rub it in such a way that the Jews, all the Jews in the world, will instantaneously become Scandinavians, without any historical memory, no martyrology, no nothing. They may become a boring people, perhaps, but they will be a happy one. Would you rub the lamp? No, I answered promptly. He did not like the speed with which I replied. He took this as an unbearable lightness toward Jewish suffering. For him suffering could never be a blessing, it was always a curse.

Basically the Jews were for him an extended family. An interesting family, possibly even a neurotic family, but by no means a "chosen" one. And, in a family like in a family: there is an adored uncle. There was indeed an uncle whom Isaiah loved. He was Isaac Landoberg, who later became Yitzhak

Sadeh, the Jewish Garibaldi, as Isaiah referred to him. Like Garibaldi, who founded the Red Shirts, Sadeh founded the Palmach, the striking units which eventually played a decisive role in Israel's War of Independence in 1948. Sadeh was not only a general, but also a writer and an essayist, and also—in his early days in Russia—a boxer, a wrestler, and an avid footballer, as well as a painter's model and an art dealer. In short, a pagan. During the Russian Revolution he came to Petrograd, as a Social Revolutionary officer, to visit the Berlins. Berlin's mother was so terrified of his huge Mauser pistol that she took it from him and put it away in a bowl of cold water, lest it explode. Sadeh ended his life in Israel as a romantic socialist. In Isaiah's eyes he remained a dazzling adventurer.

Isaiah's own family is old and intriguing. He was a direct descendant of Shneur Zalman of Liadi, the founder of the Hasidic dynasty of Lubavitch at the time of the Napoleonic wars. And in a family like in a family, there are also black sheep. A second cousin of Isaiah's was the late Lubavitcher Rebbe

Menachem Schneerson, the one whose followers in Brooklyn and elsewhere declared him to be the Messiah. Though secretly proud of his illustrious Hasidic lineage, Isaiah felt acute embarrassment with a Messiah in the family. Aline, too, has a long and no less fascinating pedigree. She was born into the family of the Barons de Gunzbourg, who distinguished themselves for three generations, up until the Russian Revolution, as grand bankers in Russia and in Paris, and were prominent in Jewish diplomacy during the pogroms against the Jews in the days of the Czars; they were also among the most pre-eminent philanthropic families in the modern history of the Jews.

And so Isaiah's family branches in all directions and it extends to the whole of the Jewish people. When Isaiah gossiped about the family it was social history at its best. And when Isaiah talked about social history it was as intimate as family gossip. It is this sense of solidarity that shaped him as the tribal cosmopolitan that he was. He had a vision of a world where people will have a sense of belonging and of identity, and in virtue of this they will have a natural sense of home so that they will be able to express their own humanity to the full.

If Jews for Isaiah meant family, what was Isaiah for the Jews? For many Jews he was Resh Galuta, Prince of the Exiles. They wanted to pay him tribute, which on many occasions meant a visit to the great man. Isaiah did not mind that in the least, not even when they were bores. He made room for everyone in his dense little diary, then met them, and enchanted them off their feet with his warmth, with his instant sense of familiarity, and above all with his mesmerizing stories.

Isaiah was a master of adjectives. He could get at the gist of one's character by a string of nuanced adjectives. There is no point in my trying to encapsulate him by adjectives: only he could have done that. So I shall end with a reminder. While remembering to mourn his death we should not forget to celebrate his life.

AVISHAI MARGALIT

Bernard Williams

- - - - -

The following address

was delivered at the

Commemoration in the

Sheldonian Theatre, Oxford,

on March 21, 1998

ISAIAH HAS BEEN much praised and discussed in the past months, and so he will be in the future. Today is itself an occasion, of course, for recalling what Isaiah did and what he stood for: and I shall try to say a little about his relations to philosophy, and to some other things as well. But we are in Oxford, where he and Aline lived for so many years and shared the warmth of their life with many other people. Here specially, when we speak of his work or his attitudes, we think first of them, and of his home, and of the way in which he was uniquely able to extend his friendship widely but not thinly.

About his relations to philosophy, the best-known thing that Isaiah said was that he gave it up—philosophy, that is to say, to use his words, "as it is taught in most English-speaking universities, and as I believe it should be taught." He said that this was the result of a conversation during the war with the Harvard logician H. M. Sheffer, who persuaded him that in philosophy one could not hope for an increase in permanent knowledge. "I gradually came to the conclusion," Isaiah wrote, "that I should prefer a field in which one could hope to know more at the end of one's life than when one had begun; and so I left philosophy for the history of ideas." He would sometimes tell a further story of how this conclusion began to force itself on him, shortly after the conversation with Sheffer, during a flight across the Atlantic in an unpressurized aircraft: he could not read, and he could not go to sleep because he was wearing an oxygen mask, and so for nine hours he had nothing to do except think, something which (he claimed) he always found exceedingly painful.

He did think that philosophy was an important and fascinating subject, which could claim transforming achievements, but he thought that they were achieved only by thinkers of genius. "Genius" was one of Isaiah's favorite words. He himself took it to be a rich and vague Romantic idea, but he applied it and withheld it with an assurance worthy of Dr. Johnson: "Wagner? undoubtedly a genius, historically a disaster"; and of almost any contemporary figure outside the sciences or the creative arts, "Genius? Certainly not." In any case, he did not regard himself as a genius. Indeed, he did not see himself as a scholar or a professionally learned man, either. When he said that he turned to the history of ideas because philosophy did not produce cumulative knowledge, he did not mean that he wanted to make great scholarly discoveries in that field or be famous for his research. He meant what he said, that he himself hoped to know more at the end of his life than when he had begun.

In fact, I do not think that he did leave philosophy. He merely left what he took philosophy to be. His conception of the subject had been formed originally by those discussions in Oxford before the war which were shaped by the agenda of positivism; and, very broadly, he stuck with that conception. The most important thing about that conception, though, so far as Isaiah was concerned, was that it saw philosophy as a timeless study, with no interest in history (except perhaps, marginally, in the history of philosophy itself). If what Isaiah wanted to do was really history, then, on this view, it could not be philosophy. Isaiah agreed with this himself, and that is why he said that he had left philosophy, and why he did not notice that he had discovered or rediscovered a different kind of philosophy, one that makes use of real history.

Analytic philosophy has been much taken up with defining things. But as Nietzsche said—not actually one of Isaiah's favorite thinkers—"one can only define things that have no history." Because that is true, all the things that Isaiah found most interesting—liberty and other political ideals, Romanticism, nationalism, ideas of individual creativity—such things do not have definitions or analyses but only complex and tangled histories, and to say what these things are, one must tell some of their history. This was what Isaiah believed, and it was expressed straightforwardly in the style of his work, in which he offered narration rather than dialectic, preferred tendencies to laws, and, in many cases, liked illustrative details best of all.

This was not just a manner or an idiosyncrasy, but expressed a quite basic idea, and it may be because of this that people have been frustrated in trying to get hold of some essence of his thought. Coming to his writings, still more to Isaiah himself, with an academic or journalistic receptacle in which they hoped to pack his principal ideas, they usually found that they had come out with too little to fill it, or too much to get into it. He, and the myriad images in his head of past worlds, of people living and dead and their thoughts, were not the right shape for receptacles.

The concrete sense which he had of the special character of different historical times was not just expressed in his philosophy. It shaped his reactions to many other things he cared about. He was notoriously impatient with opera directors who shift the historical period of the production, and just as cross when, supposedly staging the piece in the right period, they got the manners wrong. If his taste was in these ways, as the opera directors grimly pointed out, conservative, it did also conserve, and it kept alive for him materials which to a modern taste might seem psychologically or morally unconvincing. We used to discuss that crucial scene in *Traviata* in which the father tells Violetta that she must give up her affair with Alfredo because the family's reputation is being undermined by it, and she, touched by his appeal, immediately agrees; if I suggested that this does not show either of the characters in an altogether favorable light, Isaiah would have none of it, and returned me firmly to the expectations which people had in that time and place.

Isaiah's taste in opera was broad and hugely enthusiastic. What he loved most in it was sheer melody. It was Rossini, Wagner said, who had installed melody as the absolute sovereign of opera, and Isaiah's passion for Rossini was just about limitless. His relations to Wagner himself were somewhere between distant and hostile, but he did not get overexcited about the subject or give elaborate explanations of his attitude. When he invited us once to go with him to *Parsifal*, I said something to the effect that it was going to be a particularly bad evening for him: "no worse than all the others," he said.

One reason that Wagner displeased him was that his music, as Isaiah put it, "acted directly on the nerves." There were other works that also fell under this criticism, and they were in quite various styles: *Tosca* and *Turandot*, *Wozzeck*, Britten's *Peter Grimes*. I think that what these pieces had in common, and what really upset Isaiah about them, was something that always upset him very deeply, that they were too directly expressive of cruelty.

His special affection for Verdi was connected with a quality that Verdi had, which, in a famous article, Isaiah called "naiveté," in Schiller's sense: although his works very recognizably came from a particular time and place, they expressed, directly and unselfconsciously, feelings which have been experienced and understood at all times. Isaiah believed both that interesting and significant expressions of human experience are irreducibly local and peculiar, and also that in order to understand them, and to recognize the most important among them, you have to see them as rooted in understandings and powers and aspirations which in some sense are common to everybody.

These two lines of thought wound round each other in some complex ways, for instance in his attitudes to the Enlightenment. He had a basic loyalty to its reasonable ideals, which were supposed to appeal to humanity as such, but just for that reason he wanted to understand some of its darker critics and subverters. He came back continually to ways in which such conflicting ideas had shaped the experience of Russia. His favorite hero of the Enlightenment outlook was not one of its philosophers, but a man who represented it in relation to that country, off-shore, Alexander Herzen.

With most things that interested him very much, such as political ideas, it was their history that concerned him first, the particular circumstances in which they flourished. This was true, to some extent, of his interest in works of art. But when it came to the art that meant most to him, and to the works that he loved most of all, it was not true. In their case, historical relativity finally gave up, and all merely local considerations melted away. To him the works of Bach and Beethoven, Mozart and Schubert, spoke in ways to which their history, however interesting, was external and irrelevant. They were simply there, for ever, for everybody.

He shared that feeling with other people in an entirely direct and unassuming way. We shall remember his talk, and the generous way in which he talked, so that people wanted to listen to him, not simply because he was brilliant and amusing and had many things to tell them, but because he enjoyed letting them into his thoughts, and, unlike many clever talkers, had no desire to bully them or make them feel at a loss. But we shall remember him, too, when he was not talking but listening intently to this music. It will be hard, perhaps, for his friends ever to hear some of these pieces again without thinking of him, slightly bent forward, his head a little on one side, sometimes humming a bit or beating time, absorbed without a trace of self-consciousness in what for him was beyond any talk, any arguments, any history.

BERNARD WILLIAMS

Aileen
Kelly

- - - - -

The following tribute was
originally published in the
December 18, 1997, issue of
The New York Review of Books

FEW TEACHERS WILL ever be as much loved and mourned as Isaiah Berlin. As a graduate student at Wolfson College, Oxford, whose first president he became in the late 1960s, I was constantly made aware of my great luck: my choice of college within the University had brought me into the daily orbit of what we all sensed was the most fascinating, the most remarkable person we would ever encounter. Soon after I joined the College, he sent me a note asking me to come and discuss my research on the Russian intelligentsia. Out of nervousness I delayed replying until one day he descended on me at lunch, commanding me to come back with him to his office. I emerged nearly three hours later after a dazzling tour of the landscape of Russian thought

combined with a passionate vindication of the subject of my research, which others had frequently
urged me to change. In the Sixties Western liberal
academics tended to regard the Russian intelligentsia
mainly as fanatical precursors of communism. With
a warmth that recreated them as persons, Isaiah
defended them as worthy of admiration for their
moral commitment to dispelling illusions about the
world and our place in it.

Much of that afternoon we spent discussing
Alexander Herzen, whom Isaiah described as his
hero. Later that day I sought out his essays on
Herzen and came upon a precise description of my
own recent impressions:

> I was puzzled and overwhelmed, when I first
> came to know [him]—by this extraordinary
> mind which darted from one topic to another
> with unbelievable swiftness, with inexhaustible
> wit and brilliance; which could see in the turn
> of somebody's talk, in some simple incident,
> in some abstract idea, that vivid feature which

gives expression and life. He had . . . a kind of prodigal opulence of intellect which astonished his audience. . . . [His talk] demanded of those who were with him not only intense concentration, but also perpetual alertness, because you had always to be prepared to respond instantly. On the other hand, nothing cheap or tawdry could stand even half an hour of contact with him. All pretentiousness, all pompousness, all pedantic self-importance, simply fled from him or melted like wax before a fire.

Isaiah was citing a contemporary's portrait of Herzen. His own resemblance to that extraordinary figure was striking (many of us would echo, with regard to Isaiah, Tolstoy's comment on Herzen— that he had never met anyone with "so rare a combination of scintillating brilliance and depth"), but his sense of affinity with Herzen was based above all on a shared moral outlook. They both combined a deep respect for honesty and purity of motivation with an unerring ability to detect artificiality and self-deception in intellectual endeavor and everyday behavior. Students sensed that with Isaiah they were not required to perform, amuse, or entertain, but simply to give their best, and this paradoxically put us at ease with him, the more so as we soon found out that straining to impress him was counterproductive. (Once, hoping to be congratulated on the originality of an essay I had given him for comment, I was chagrined to find that he had read the footnotes just as closely as the text and had unearthed some errors of fact which I had overlooked in my haste to impress.)

Isaiah's personality and utterances were the subject of continual discussion by the students of his College. His Russian connections and his exotic past provided much food for inventive speculation: Had the unusual circular hole in his ancient felt hat been acquired during hostile action somewhere in the Baltic states? More than once he walked unexpectedly into a room where a passable imitation of his own unforgettable voice was in full flow.

I believe that his true voice can be found at its clearest in his essays on Herzen. More self-revealing than anything else he ever wrote, they shed light on the most enduring mystery about him: his combination of what many have seen as a tragic vision of the world with an inexhaustible curiosity and an irrepressible sense of fun.

Isaiah can be said to have rediscovered Herzen, who he believed had either been ignored or misrepresented for so long because he had revealed a truth too bleak for most people to bear: that faith in universally valid formulas and goals was an attempt to escape from the unpredictability of life into the false security of fantasy. His devotion to Herzen remained undiminished to the end of his life. Not long ago he wrote reproaching me for obscuring the uniqueness of Herzen's contribution by drawing parallels between him and thinkers such as Mikhail Bakhtin who had considered similar problems: "I can think of none, but perhaps I am too fanatical an admirer." He often cited Herzen's phrase "history has no libretto": all questions make sense and must be resolved not in terms of final goals but of the specific needs of actual persons at specific times and places. Herzen, he wrote, believed "that the day and the hour were ends in themselves, not a means to another day or another experience."

Here we have the key to one of the central paradoxes of Isaiah. Although his diary was always full and he was scrupulous about keeping appointments, he never gave the impression of being in a hurry, of being distracted from a person or an issue by anticipation of the next person or problem in line. Young academics were often astonished (as I was in my first encounter with him) that so important and busy a man was prepared to give them so much of his time. An American Slavist whom I met recently at a conference recalled having sent him her first book, not expecting a reply. His warm and detailed response, she told me, had her walking on air for weeks. On the evening after his death I remembered him with a Russian colleague whom he had encouraged in the same way in Oxford many years ago. A "*svetlaia lichnost*" (luminous personality), she said.

But we would diminish him if we did not appreciate that the instinctive goodness we loved was coupled with a carefully thought-through moral vision of whose validity he earnestly sought to persuade us. One of its distinctive characteristics, which he saw embodied in Herzen, was the total absence of a utilitarian approach to people and events, an "unquenchable delight in the variety of life and the comedy of human character." This was also one of Isaiah's most entrancing qualities. I remember him as the only one of us to emerge unexasperated from an interminable and contentious College meeting, happily quoting Kant's statement that "from the crooked timber of humanity no straight thing can ever be made." He was convinced (again I quote him on Herzen) that there was value in the very irregularity of the structure of human beings, "which is violated by attempts to force it into patterns or straitjackets."

Like Herzen (and Schiller) he believed profoundly in the seriousness of the play of life and human creativity, and was easily drawn into all kinds of frivolity. One night after dinner at Wolfson he joined a conversation in which a student was explaining the board game Diplomacy, where each player represented one of the Great Powers of pre-1914 Europe. He invited us to his house the following Sunday morning to initiate him into the game; he then gave an impressively illiberal performance as the Ottoman Empire.

I have another memory of him sitting on a bale of hay in his three-piece suit, complete with watch chain and hat, holding forth to a group of fascinated students at a bonfire party held in a damp field on the bank of the Cherwell, where the building of the new College was to start the next day. It was late evening; a more typical college president, having put in the obligatory early appearance, would have been long gone.

All those who knew him well were asked over the years to persuade him to write more and not to squander his gifts in conversation. Yet his profligacy has not prevented him from being recognized as one of the major liberal thinkers of the twentieth century, and he belongs to an even more select group who achieved harmony between their moral vision and their life. He showed us virtue in action, not as

obedience to a set of rules but as a generous respon-
siveness to the creative possibilities of the present
moment. One always came away from a few hours
in his company with a sense of living more intensely,
with all one's perceptions heightened, although the
topics of conversation were often far from exalted.
He much enjoyed exchanging news about the latest
academic scandals in Oxford and Cambridge, and
expected the exchange to be on equal terms: his
view of humanity required that Cambridge should
be as fertile a source of stories about human frailty
as Oxford, and he was never disappointed. We had
an unfinished debate lasting several years over the
precise difference between a cad and a bounder; he
could always find fresh examples of each to offer
from among our mutual acquaintances.

He loved to gossip about the concerns and quar-
rels of nineteenth-century Russian thinkers as though
they were our common friends, but there was a seri-
ous side to this entertainment. He had the greatest
respect for these thinkers' commitment to acting
out their beliefs in their daily lives, and fiercely

championed them against what he perceived as misjudgments of their motives; our one painful difference was over the question of how Turgenev would have behaved under particular pressures.

Isaiah saw no contradiction between recognizing that moral ideals were not absolute and believing one's own ideals binding on oneself. Again, his model was Herzen, who, he tells us, for all his skepticism, had an unshakable belief in the sanctity of personal liberty and the noble instincts of the human soul, as well as a hatred of "conformism, cowardice, submission to the tyranny of brute force or pressure of opinion, arbitrary violence, and anxious submissiveness . . . the worship of power, blind reverence for the past, for institutions, for mysteries or myths; the humiliation of the weak by the strong, sectarianism, philistinism, the resentment and envy of majorities, the brutal arrogance of minorities." Here, albeit in the third person, is Isaiah's profession of faith, in his own cadences.

He admired Herzen more than Turgenev because while neither had any illusions about the permanence of human existence and human values, Turgenev had achieved a cool detachment from the struggles and triumphs of contingent life, while Herzen "cared far too violently"; his realism was therefore the more courageous. In his last years Isaiah confronted the tragic side of his own philosophy with the same unflinching directness as his hero. On arriving for dinner in Cambridge sixteen months ago, he told me that something "very terrible" concerning him had just appeared in the press. He would say no more about it and I assumed it was some adverse review. The next day I found the interview, reprinted in the London *Times*, in which he reflects on his own death, declaring that, much though he would like it to be otherwise, the idea that there was some world in which there would be perfect truth, love, justice, and happiness made no sense in any conceptual scheme he knew. It was just a comforting idea for people who could not face the possibility of total extinction. But, he adds, "I wouldn't mind living on and on.... I am filled with curiosity and long to know, what next?"

ABOUT THE TYPE

The text type, Sabon, was designed by the son of a letter-painter, Jan Tschichold (1902–1974), who was jointly commissioned in 1960, by Monotype, Linotype, and Stempel, to create a typeface which would produce consistent results when produced by hand-setting, or with either the Monotype or Linotype machines.

The German book designer and typographer is known for producing a wide range of designs. Tschichold's early work, considered to have revolutionized modern typography, was influenced by the avant-garde Bauhaus and characterized by bold asymmetrical sans serif faces. With his Sabon design, Tschichold demonstrates his later return to more formal and traditional typography. Sabon is based upon the roman Garamond face of Konrad Berner, who married the widow of printer Jacques Sabon. The italic Sabon is modeled after the work of Garamond's contemporary, Robert Granjon.

In Sabon, Tschichold's appreciation of classical letters melds with the practicality of consistency and readability into a sophisticated and adaptable typeface.

Sabon is a registered trademark of
Linotype-Hell AG and/or its subsidiaries

Printed and bound by R. R. Donnelley & Sons,
Harrisonburg, Virginia

Jacket and Book Design by
Red Canoe, Deer Lodge, TN
Caroline Kavanagh
Deb Koch